SELECTED F

FRANK THOMPSON

Edited by Dorothy and Kate Thompson
with an introduction by Dorothy Thompson

TRENT EDITIONS

Published by Trent Editions 2003

Trent Editions
Department of English and Media Studies
The Nottingham Trent University
Clifton Lane.
Nottingham NG11 8NS

Printed in Great Britain by Goaters Limited, Nottingham

Cover: Photograph of Frank Thompson, taken during World War Two

ISBN 1 84233 070 5

Contents

Introduction

William Frank Thompson was born in Darjeeling, India, on 18 August 1920. He was named after his maternal grandfather, William Jessup and his father's younger brother, Frank who had been killed three years earlier on the Western front. His father, Edward John Thompson had served as a Methodist chaplain in the Mesopotamian campaign where he had been awarded the Military Cross. His mother, Theodosia Jessup came from a family of American Presbyterian missionaries who were associated with the American College in Beirut. She had been teaching French and Arabic to Red Cross personnel in Jerusalem when she had met Edward. From his earliest years Frank grew up in an international atmosphere. He visited and lived as a young child in India, the Lebanon and the Unites States. From 1923 onwards the family was based in Oxford where Edward held a post as lecturer in Bengali and later became an honorary fellow of Oriel College.

Both parents maintained their contacts and many friendships with India and with the Lebanon, and the Oxford house received many visitors from both countries and from the United States. Neighbours included Robert Graves and Nancy Nicholson, whose children were of an age to be regular playmates of the Thompson boys and who remained their friends throughout their lives. Frank and his younger brother, the historian E.P. Thompson, went as day boys to the Dragon School, described by the latter as 'a robust, elite preparatory school in which proficiency in Greek and Latin was the only benchmark of scholastic excellence'.[1] Frank soon became proficient in classical and modern languages and developed a passion for languages and for literature which remained with him throughout his life. As a schoolboy he spent holidays in Europe, including a summer spent at an archaeological dig in Crete, where he was able to gain a knowledge of modern Greek to add to his familiarity with the classical language.

The Thompsons were, and are, a family of writers. Edward senior was a poet, novelist, historian, biographer and writer of serious and influential journalism. Theodosia published plays and journalism. Her father William Jessup was the author of a two-volume autobiography while Edward junior, writing as E.P. Thompson to distinguish himself from his father, later became one of the most influential historians of his generation. Frank expressed himself in writing from his earliest years. He left behind letters diaries and journals covering most of his life, and was writing and reading poetry from his early childhood. By the time he went as a scholar to Winchester College in 1933, he was already immersed in the study of languages and the writing of verse. Freeman Dyson, the physicist, who was at Winchester at the same time, remembered Frank's organizing Russian classes and promoting enthusiasm for the study of the language and literature, He also recalled his lifelong commitment to poetry:

> From him I caught my first inkling of the great moral questions of
> war and peace that were to dominate our lives ever afterwards.
> Listening to him talking I learnt that there is no way to rightly
> grasp these great questions except through poetry. For him poetry was
> no mere intellectual amusement. Poetry was man's best effort down
> the ages to distil some wisdom from the inarticulate depths of his
> soul. Frank could no more live without poetry than I could live
> without mathematics.[2]

Theirs was a generation which grew up in the shadow of the Great War of 1914-1918 and under the threat of the renewed European conflict that was to break out in 1939. Frank had just reached call-up age when war was declared, and had by that time been involved in the increasing tensions dividing Europe from the time of the outbreak of the Spanish war in 1936. Neighbours at Oxford included the Carritt family, whose five sons were close friends of Frank and Edward. Two of the brothers, Noel and Anthony, volunteered to serve in the International Brigade in support of the Spanish government, and Anthony, who served as an ambulance driver, was killed there. The Carritt sons and their mother were members of the Communist Party, but Frank did not join until he was an undergraduate. He did, however, put in some hard work in support of A.D. Lindsay, the master of Balliol, who stood in a Parliamentary bye-election in October 1938 as an anti-appeasement candidate, supported by an ad hoc group of liberal and left-wing activists against the Chamberlain-ite Tory, Quentin Hogg (later Lord Hailsham). Lindsay lost by a narrow majority, and Frank recalled in one of the series of 'snapshots of Oxford' which he wrote two years later, the disappointment of the Lindsay supporters when Hogg's victory was announced

> We felt glum that night at the Hollywell gate. The October air should

have been a stimulus but we were like rags soaked in cold vinegar. Obscurantism had triumphed. Some one grew bitter 'I hope North Oxford gets the first bombs. But it would be tough on the pekineses.' Michael looked fiercely at the ground, pulled his collar up round his neck as if it was a gown and made a pronouncement. 'There are only two alternatives now—to join the Communist Party or abdicate from politics. I can't swallow communism so I'll abdicate and take up psychology.'

Frank himself was persuaded by Iris Murdoch to join the communist party early the following year. They were part of a group of close student friends in the year of the outbreak of war whose story has been sensitively told by Peter Conradi in his recent biography of Iris.[3] By the time Frank went into the army at the end of the year his relationship with Iris was close although perhaps one of emotional and intellectual friendship rather than sexual involvement. It was in his letters to Iris, though, as well as those to his brother and his parents, that he wrote about his deepest feelings while he was on active service; some of the poems in this collection are taken from a file of typed and manuscript versions which was among Iris's papers and which was probably a selection he had made for her from his work.

European communism in the late nineteen thirties was centrally concerned with opposition to imperialism and resistance to Fascism. Both these world evils seemed to be functions of late capitalism in the West, where an economic depression was producing violent, authoritarian and racist regimes. The Soviet Union represented for many an area of the world where the profit motive had been eliminated and the country set upon the road to cooperative and peaceful growth. The authoritarianism of dogmatic communism was seen as a stage in the modernization of a backward and rural economy, a stage that might not be needed in the conversion to socialism of an advanced industrial nation This is a simplified and compressed summary of the motivation of the men and women in the communist movement who risked unpopularity and victimisation even in Britain, and in parts of Europe persecution, exile and prison or concentration camp. During the war years the resistance of the Soviets to the Nazi onslaught and the leading part played in the European resistance movements reinforced Communist and Socialist ideas.

The British Communist Party famously changed its line overnight from support for the war against Germany to its denunciation as an 'imperialist conflict'. Frank had volunteered for service immediately upon the declaration of war, and although his parents at first managed to get him released because he was under age, he insisted on remaining in the service. A poem written to Iris, 'Madonna Bolshevika', explained his position:

Sure, lady, I know the party line is better
I know what Marx would have said. I know you're right
When this is over we'll fight for the things that matter
Somehow to-day I simply want to fight.

He was commissioned in 1940 in the Royal Artillery. He served with the GHQ Liaison regiment, known as 'Phantom', where he was mainly concerned with information gathering in Libya, Persia, Iran and finally Sicily. He volunteered for the Special Operations Executive in late 1943, at first hoping to be sent to Greece, but later opting for the Bulgarian mission. His diaries of the training including the parachute jumping are a vivid record of some of the preparation which volunteers for this work went through.

The SOE Bulgarian project was code-named 'Claridges'. It was a small group of men under the command of Major Mostyn Davies who were to work as liaison officers with the Bulgarian partisans organizing weapons drops and other forms of support and guidance. The story of the ill-fated mission has been told several times.[4] None of these accounts is complete, since the records are in some cases still not available to historians, in others are distorted by personal and political interests. The most complete account is the one given by E.P. Thompson in his Camp lectures of 1981,[5] but he was very much aware when he prepared these from the then available material that the full story remained to be told. Since the lectures were published, more research in Bulgaria has added to the account of the capture and death of Frank and the partisans with him. The original Bulgarian version had included a mock trial in which Frank had proclaimed himself a communist and defied the authorities. In fact it now seems that the group was shot as they were walking away under the direction of their captors so that they might have been described as 'shot whilst trying to escape' rather than executed.

At the time of his capture and death Frank Thompson was serving as a British liaison officer, not, as one author has suggested, as an 'agent'. He was following orders in a situation of confused and distorted communications. The attempted partisan action which he had been instructed to support was one with at best a limited possibility of development. It seems to have been caught in the cross-fire of high-level negotiations between the western Allies, the Soviet Union and the Axis powers. The small group of two officers and accompanying wireless operator and interpreters was assembled at first on the Jugoslav side of the border with Bulgaria. This was an area of intense partisan activity and before they could cross the frontier Mostyn Davies was killed in an ambush from which only Frank escaped. The partisans on that side of the frontier were strong enough to protect him and to allow the mission to regroup. He was now the senior officer and had to make the decision to cross the frontier when the partisans were ready to move. His decision to go forward with the detachment was not that of a romantic adventurist, but was in line with the instructions under which he was acting.

Partisan activity in Bulgaria was much more limited than that in some other areas of the Balkans. Although Bulgaria was allied to the Axis powers, it was not at war with the Soviet Union. The strong affinity between Russia and Bulgaria dating from the days of the Ottoman Empire would have made war with Russia a difficult policy to enforce. Nevertheless the Bulgarian military were used to help hold down the resistance movement in Jugoslavia and there was a strong military presence within the country, which was not that of an occupying power. There was little support for partisan action in the countryside and the instructions which were being received from the émigré communist leadership in Moscow were from urban communists long absent from their country and never familiar with the peasantry. The Western allies were negotiating with the Bulgarian government, hoping to bring the whole country away from the axis, and therefore at best lukewarm in their attitude towards a revolutionary communist-led guerilla uprising. The contingent was betrayed, and finally ambushed and captured after a long trek through the countryside. Although a British officer in uniform, Frank Thompson was shot with the partisans. The story of the mission has been told in a number of ways. In the early years of the post-war communist regime Frank was presented as a heroic figure, a British communist ant-fascist fighter who had died with his Bulgarian comrades in the common struggle. A small railway station near where they were captured was named the Major Thompson station and his mother and brother were feted by the government when they went to its opening in 1947. After the split between Tito and the Soviet authorities in 1948, the official story became that the British mission had been agents trying to divert the Bulgarian partisans away from their natural protectors into the camp of western capitalism. In those years names, including Frank's, were removed from monuments and museums. In the seventies when the atmosphere in the Balkans began to thaw, renewed approaches to Britain were made. Old partisans were coming back into favour and there was a project to make a film about the partisan movement in which the British officers, Frank in particular, were to appear as heroic figures. A film crew came to England in the summer of 1977 and made a short documentary about Frank. Family, friends and colleagues were filmed recalling their memories of him and of the failed expedition. With the film makers came Slavcho Trunsky, who had been the commander of another partisan brigade and who now, after a period in disgrace, was again back in favour – indeed was a full general and a member of the government. His contribution to the film was only partly translated into English and was clearly repeating the story that the original mission and Mostyn Davies in particular, were not intended to support the partisans but to contain them.[5] By the time Edward and I visited Bulgaria in 1979 the country was anxious to improve relations with Britain and some of the monuments had been restored and the name of Frank Thompson carved into some of the war memorials. In 1994 when I visited Bulgaria for the ceremony of remembrance on the fiftieth anniversary of the death of Frank and the partisans, I was told by a Bulgarian that the British liaison officers had first been presented to them as heroic allies in the fight against fascism, then as imperialist agents infiltrating on behalf of the western allies and then, after 1989, as Soviet agents intent on establishing Soviet hegemony. There are lessons for historians here.

In 1994 on the fiftieth anniversary of the death of Frank and his comrades a ceremony was held at the monument to them near the village of Litakovo where they had died. The British ambassador and the British defence attaché spoke and laid wreaths, as did the Bulgarian Commander of the First Army, representing Bulgarian armed forces. English and Bulgarian versions of two poems, 'Sharing' by the Bulgarian Poet Christo Botev and 'Polliticii Meliora' by Frank Thompson, were read before the Last Post was sounded.

Acknowledgements

These poems were written between 1928 and 1944. They are the work of a very young man who did not live long enough to revise and re-work them for publication. A few have been published in collections (see the notes following the poems for further information). The selection has been made by Frank's niece, Kate Thompson, herself a poet and writer. We have been helped in producing this volume by a number of people. Tony Foster, a school friend of Frank and a lifelong friend of his brother and his family has helped with advice and encouragement. Simon Kusseff who is working on the biography has been enormously helpful in providing information of many kinds. Peter Conradi through his work on Iris Murdoch has come to understand Frank probably better than any one of his generation and has provided in his book an account which will give any interested reader a fuller and more nuanced account of him than is possible here.

Neither Kate nor I are classical scholars and we have been very grateful to Mary Midgely and Roland Mayer for reading the poems for us to see whether any are direct translations from the classical verse which was such an important part of Frank's intellectual landscape. Our thanks also to Desmond Costa and Cathy Porter for generous help in locationg and translating references.

Notes

1. E.P. Thompson, *Beyond the Frontier* (London and Stanford, USA, 1997), p. 50.
2. Freeman Dyson, *Disturbing the Universe* (London, 1981), p. 35.
3. Peter Conradi, *Iris Murdoch: A Life* (London, 2001).
4. E.P. Thompson and T.J. Thompson (eds) *There is a Spirit in Europe* (London, 1947; second edition revised 1948); Stowers Johnson, *Agents Extraordinary* (London. 1975); Thompson, Beyond the Frontier; Peter Conradi, *Iris Murdoch: a Life* (2001) pp 82-196 and *passim*.
5. The 35mm copy of the film is now in the British Film Institute.

I POEMS 1935–1939

DEATH IN THE MINES

Lords of the earth, for you our lives we gave,
Not, as in war, that others might be killed;
But, in the darkness, found a living grave
To warm your hearths and keep your cellars filled.

DEATH IN THE MOUNTAINS

These in the wild serenity of snow
Communion held with God. Weep not for these,
But for the sluggards in the town below,
Who dared not meet their lord with souls at ease.

December 1935

"WAR SO JUNG UND MORGENSCHÖN"[1]

Spring on his brow – and in his heart was spring;
He left us in the April of his years.
He does not ask for sighing or for tears,
Who left when it was still worth lingering,
Before the autumn winds, which rise and bring
Like fallen leaves a whirl of fleeting fears,
And Doubt with harsh iconoclastic jeers.
He died when Death had still a dreadful ring.

No, not for him, but others we must moan,
Whom April's blooms, too early withering,
Left vainly groping in a darkened maze.
Their cheeks are still with roses all ablaze,
But in their hearts grim clouds are gathering
– November fog, that chills them to the bone.

December 1936

LOVE UNRECIPROCATE

Of course you could not love me; love, to live,
Must have some solid object, anchor'd fast.
A jade, a wanderer, you could not love,
Whose only aim is sleep. From joy outcast,

Nor yet of sorrow's kingdom, here I roam,
Chasing the gilded butterflies of hell.
No wonder that you could not find me room,
In all your heart, to soothe and make me well.

Where shall I find a harbour for my soul
Against the storm-toss'd drifting of the main?
You might have been that harbour. – Now I sail
Far out beyond the breakers once again.

One day you too will wake, as I have woken;
You too will feel alone; then sympathise,
Rememb'ring one, whose love, in time, will weaken,
But not his loneliness until he dies.

May 1937

RESIGNATION

Leave here my Hope, my broken flyer,
    Whose first trip was her last.
She was not built for storms; her engine
    Chok'd in the strong, cold blast.

Pedestrian from now, – mechanic –
    Look on while others fly.
Sweat but no glory – why not better
    Admit defeat and die?

No. Though my search for stars soon ended
    In flames across the sky,
In earth's cool waking I discover'd
    I did not want to die.

4

Bruis'd but at rest, in deep green clover,
    Heart beating hard with earth,
I found it was not stars but flowers
    Presided at my birth.

July 1937

LINES TO A COMMUNIST FRIEND

Here, in the tranquil fragrance of the honeysuckle,
The gentle, soothing velvet of the foxgloves,
The cuckoo's drowsy laugh, – I thought of you,
The ever-whirring dynamos of your will,
Body and brain one swift, harmonious strength,
Flashing like polished steel to rid the world
Of all its gross unfairness. – But the grossest
Unfairness of it all is that, tomorrow,
When both of us are gone, my sloth, your energy,
The world will still be cruelly perverse.
  – Why not enjoy the foxgloves, while they last?

July 1937

TO A COMMUNIST FRIEND

A year ago, in the drowsy Vicarage garden,
We talked of politics; you, with your tawny hair
Flamboyant, flaunting your red tie, unburden'd
Your burning heart of the dirge we always hear –
The rich triumphant and the poor oppress'd.
And I laugh'd, seeing, I thought, an example
Of vague ideals not tried but taken on trust,
That would not stand the test. It sounded all too simple.

A year has pass'd; and now, where harsh winds rend
The street's last shred of comfort, – past the dread
Of bomb or gunfire, rigid on the ground
Of some cold stinking alley near Madrid,
Your mangled body festers, – an example
Of something tougher. – Yet it still sounds all too simple.

December 1937

O CUR JUBES CANERE? [2]

You are kind, very kind to me, lady;
    But you wouldn't understand.
A song, I'm afraid, is impossible
    In this strange land.

I know that the waters of Babylon
    Are faster, more turbid with foam:
The glamour and rhythm are better
    Than they were at home.

The men and the methods of Babylon
    Are more efficient than ours.
They have pride in their roaring engines
    And their strong high towers.

But something I loved in Jerusalem,
    A charm which you could not know;
Yes, something is missing from Babylon
    For all its show.

That peaceful beauty has vanished,
    That easy wistful smile,
The gentle humorous tolerance
    That made life worth while.

You are kind, very kind to me, lady;
    Please try to understand
Why I cannot sing the old melodies
    In this new strange land.
                        February 1938?

MY EPITAPH

Here in the sunlit cloister let your mirth
    Blend and suffuse my last and sweetest rest.
Laughter and sleep were all I loved on earth;
    And now I find the latter far the best.

February 1938

ON THE EXTINCTION OF AUSTRIA

Now that the new spring blood
Rushes out with joy from the heart,
And the hand grows keen to war and the fingers to fight,
In this radiant morning heat
You ask why we take to flight,
Not following up the sporadic barrage of insults
With the steady advance of the thunder'd Wordsworthian sonnet
Till we sweep the field with scorn?
Seeing the trenches abandon'd,
The rifles rusty and rotting,
You ask why no sonnet is born?

The time for resistance is past.
Not a cause but an aeon is dead.
An age, not a nation is plunged in the final darkness
Of the storm-cloud's smothering dread.
And Man, whose planes once rode
Strong-wing'd the soul's empyrean,
Has shudder'd and plunged through an agony of silence
And now with all his shatter'd hopes lies buried
In the State's grand mausoleum:
The new tempo is too hurried
For all but the mad to mourn.
And so, while strong boots trample
Spring's violets in the mud,
We can only retreat and grumble.
That last frost was too cruel;
It has frozen the new spring blood.

March 1938

THE PARTHENON FLOODLIT

Below, the clustered jewelry of the city
Stretches out with a myriad sparkles across the plain
From Parnes to Pendell. On the hill
Gleam the Doric columns of a different age:
But the difference is gone. Rejuvenated,
But still at peace, they have entered a glaring field,
Forgetting old glories and sorrows batteries,
With the neon sign and the lighted office building,
And the victory is sure. In this new strange Babel
They rule with the same unchallenged serenity
As they did when the city was young and the men who throng'd her
Were younger too and had beauty in their hearts.

April 1938

DEMOCRAT'S DEFEAT

Leaving behind in the plains
The massed battalions of death,
The formic manoeuvres of black and brown and scarlet,
Let us strike to the hills for breath.

Why look back with regret
At the war-dance if dupe and slave,
In the adventitious strength of collective hysteria,
On the individual's grave?

Rise up with the sun in your heart!
It will fade forever too soon.
Rise up and challenge with fruitless fury the gods!
But make sure that you do it alone.

Some will gutter and faint in an hour.
Some will crash at last in the flames,
Having blazed for a while on the sky and men's hearts amazement
At the radiance of their fame.

But the gulf between glory and silence
Is minute, if one knew the truth.
In the end it will be enough to have remembered
One's strength in the days of one's youth.

May 1938

AURELIAN IN THE PROTESTANT CEMETERY

Within the walls I built to keep them out
The Northern raiders lie: beyond them lie
The buildings they made ruins, once my pride.
They swept down like the north wind, fierce and cold,
And struck my city shivering; then the tide
Roar'd back, and ebbing left
Seeds of my new beauty richer than the old.

Age mellow'd them: but Tiber's mud had swirl'd
Ten centuries since the last time, when they hurl'd
Defiance once again. This time was strange,
Far stranger than the last one, and the fight
On both sides bloody: Let the kindly flood
Of Lethe drown and hide it from our sight.

And now by my old walls they lie and sleep,
Beneath the older pyramid, and they
Are old now too and drowsy: let them stay,
Now they have made their enemy their home.
Sleep well. In those few Northern hearts was stor'd
More sun than ever beat its rays on Rome.

June 1938

DEATH OF LYKAON (*ILIAD* XXI 107-113)

"Even Patroklos died and I must die.
  Morning or evening or at blazing noon,
With pointed spear or skilful archery,
  My fate will come, is coming, all too soon."

Small comfort to the dying. Each cold word
Crept nearer to the last that he would hear.
He, sadly inattentive, only heard
The laughter of boys in meadows, where last year
He played, and left too early; Ida's streams;
The old men shrill as crickets on Troy's wall;
Then silence rolling in upon his dreams.

The Hero grasped his sword; he saw it rise
To challenge the sun's splendour, felt it fall,
And then the mist closed down about his eyes.

August 1938

IN THE ACROPOLIS MUSEUM

That was the hardest struggle, seeing the lion's strength
Stretched out from head to haunches – all its length
One glorious rhythmic curve above its prey.
And with the sight sneaked back the old heresy,
Sapping the blood from my stomach, making me dizzy
 – "How does this square with your flabby philosophy
Of tolerance and peace? Is the highest beauty
After all in the lion's sinews, the hawk's keen swiftness?
Is the greatest good the hunter's victory?"

But the answer was at hand; on the hill outside
Shone a beauty that silenced all. Timeworn but timeless,
Smiling with quiet sadness over Greece,
Stood the goddess of wisdom's temple. The lion's pride,
The eagle swooping, – both vanished to snakelike symbols
Before the full-blooded splendour of that Peace.

August 1938

10

THE NORMAN IN EXILE

On these idyllic shores of citron-bloom,
Here in this land of blue unclouded sky,
This languid land of death, I long for home,
Hating these fragrant hill-slopes, hard and dry
With crystalline negation. Leaving these,
Let me go once more to my home town in the hills,
The mountains wild with dark facades of trees,
The smooth, green pastures and their ceaseless bells.

Gods of the Hyperboreans, you who came
Southward and lost, like me, in all but name,
Grant me, returning to that upland town,
To stride those hills, wind-flouted and cloud-kissed,
And hear the Northern torrents thunder down
From Northern mountains wrapped in Northern mist.

                                    Lasithi – May 1938

UNTITLED

The night and I are one: this empty street
Has lost its meaning: nothing more exists:
Odd couples, buses, houses, sickly lights
Are fading out – the raindrop's subtle beat
Reality's last link. And you, my love,
Were like this night. I had known other nights
Laughing with stars, that snatched me up above
For one brief drunken rapture, flung me back
For cynic dawn to mock at. – None, like this,
Had ever raised me gently to her breast,
Had steeped me in the nectar of her tears,
And with the tender sadness of her kiss
Smoothed out the ugly wrinkles of my fears.

                                    January 1939

VAL D'ISERE

Yesterday late in the evening we sat up talking,
Morbidly filling our glasses, draining them slowly:
We wondered whether true happiness really existed
Except for the savage, and that, perhaps, quite bestial:
There was talk, I remember, of Rousseau and Aristotle,
And you, I think, quoted Faust.
And then you were angry with me, branding me soulless,
Because I took little interest, went to bed early.

But now, this morning, standing high on the snow-ridge,
Watching the sky clear blue behind the mountains,
Hearing the silence of snow and sunshine blending,
I'm lord of all your theories. This morning
Is not an isolated point, soon passing,
But is fused in my blood and brain with other mornings
Bursting in glory over flow'ring orchards,
Long afternoons of buttercups and swallows,
Sunsets and nights. All these ferment and ripen,
Grow part of me, then rise on rain-bound evenings
With wine-vitality and set me reeling.

January 1939

WATCHING MY CYNTHIA LISTENING TO A LARK.

Watching my Cynthia listening to a lark,
I felt in my heart a new and more bitter sadness.
The sight of her keen face keyed to the spring's clear music
Reminded me of the old self that I had buried,
And a time when Spring had given to me the same life.

Yet the dregs of the bitterness were that I thought for a moment
That she had the power to revive that old self with her freshness.
Success looked so near.
But between the past and the present
Styx and the Rubicon roll. And I had forgotten.

March 1939

EPITAPH ON A CHRISTIAN NATIONALIST

With Moorish troops I sacked the towns of Spain;
    With German planes I ground the Basques to dust,
And bombed their Holy City. – Why complain
    About the means? My ends were right, I trust.

AN EPITAPH ON DR GOEBBELS

In life I made my blue-eyed, Aryan land
Hellish, and, give me credit, did it well.
But now, of course, I'm sure you'll understand,
I shan't be up to Aryanising Hell.
                  February 1939?

SPAIN

And so the first round has finished
In the triumph of lusts and fears;
Sad end to the sad overture
Of breaking hearts and spears.
And the cold winds whisper drily across the sierras
That again free men have been enslaved and murdered;
Murmur that we have betrayed another friend.

For them a retreat, a pause;
For us a grim beginning.
We shall enter, the new protagonists,
Not forgetting, not forgiving:
That in time the winds may whisper across the sierras
"At last they are coming to give you the freedom they owe you.
Very late, very late they remember to help their friends."
                  April 1939

II POEMS 1939–1940

OMMATUR D'AN ACHYNIAIS

I, who had thought the cynic will had power,
Allied with sceptic Time, to slur and dim
The mind's clear image, hoped each laughing hour
Would near my flagging passion to the rim
    Of Lethe's drowsy lake, must not recant,
    Nor cease from longing for the adamant.

That was a year ago. And yesterday
Some girl with eyes like yours, some chance remark
Like yours serenely vague – my memory lay
Sullen as powder waiting for the spark.
    It blazed, but meeting only air and stone
    Sank down and left me, shivering and alone.

April 1939

TO A STATESMAN

Has no sound pierced through the walls of your dream-city,
In a break between vapid banquet and pompous meeting,
No voice edged in through the mob's hysterical greeting,
To dim that complacent smile of crocodile pity?

You have heard, perhaps, here and there, impossible prattle
Of twisted limbs, bombed cities, and children shrieking,
The brute suppression of truth, men shot for speaking,
And here, in this country, men dying, and living, like cattle.

You have even heard, now and then, a disquieting rumour
Of the mind's slow torture, the sadist's maniacal leer,
Cold hunger rotting the will, and hunted fear.
But you smile: You've kept your English sense of humour.

Would you smile, if you open'd a little your city's gate
And saw outside the darkening swell of hate?

May 1939

TO IRUSHKA AT THE COMING OF WAR[3]

If you should hear my name among those killed,
Say you have lost a friend, half man, half boy,
Who, if the years had spared him might have built
Within him courage strength and harmony
Uncouth and garrulous his tangled mind
Seething with warm ideas of truth and light,
His help was worthless. Yet had fate been kind
He might have learned to steel himself and fight.
He thought he loved you. By what right could he
Claim such high praise, who only felt his frame
Riddled with burning lead, and failed to see
His own false pride behind the barrel's flame?
    Say you have lost a friend and then forget.
    Stronger and truer ones are with you yet.
                                            10th July 1939

DEFEAT

Foolish, this morning, fired with corporate glow
Of something beyond myself, I dared to think
That I lived for my faith, to strike for my faith some blow,
For those ideals that we value more than life.
I thought it, and I believed it. – But evening ended,
I'm feeling tired; the world is still unmended;
And you aloof. My brain begins to cry
What my blood has always known, but I deny:
That for this alone have I been striving,
That this might be the end of all my fighting,
 – To feel your hair caress my cheeks, and rest
Till death on the soft fullness of your breast.
                                            July 1939

LE REVENANT[1]

Yes. It was all the same – the rain-dark towers,
Sulking above the autumn-sodden meads;
The lazy river, scornful of the hours,
Soothing the placid trout beneath its weeds.

The faces I knew or thought I knew;
The scarlet vestments of the cheerful choir,
The kindly men who framed me as I grew;
The fat old canon dozing by the fire.

Just for a moment, as I crossed their track,
They took my hand and smiled, as if to say
"How strange that we'd forgotten" – then turned back,
Their surface hardly rippled, on their way.

    I, who was counted once a part of this,
    Knew, like a ghost, my utter emptiness.
                  Winchester, November 1939

TO F.D.S.S.M.[5]

Together, my friend,
We smiled at death in the evening,
Recalling the goodness of grey stones and laughter;
Knowing how little either of us mattered,
We found a kind of happiness, if not peace.

You went, my friend,
To spread your wings on the morning;
I to the gun's cold elegance; and one
  – Did you feel too the passing of a shadow
Between the glasses? – one will not return.
                  9th December 1939

CAMILLA

Calm in your hair the sunlight rests and dreams;
Fierce in your eyes the fire of vision gleams.
From all the men of your brave company
Friendship you have and silent loyalty.

Fighter and mystic — still you wait for one
Noblest of all men, who shall take in fee
No glancing kiss like green Endymion
But all your laughing warm vitality.

January 1st 1940

KYRANA

"Who was the god you met in the woods alone?"

"No virgin god with frayed grey beard of stone.
No thorn-worn anguish-god of skin and bone.
A lordly god, full-blooded and full-blown.

"A lion-god, hawk-sighted and hawk-free,
Who wrestled with still greater strength than me,
Whose lyre outsang the lark's lucidity —
Only to him would I yield mastery."

February 1940

A PRAYER

A pointless picture, Satan,
But *you* should understand –
My love, the white cyclamen,
And the wine-red stains.

Help me to find her, Satan,
Graceful and tough,
And she would laugh at my complexities
And soothe my pains.
Had I a soul to barter,
Were *she* enough?
No! But you bought it long ago
And what remains?

Help me to find her, quickly,
In this brainless, artless land –
My love, the white cyclamen,
And the wine-red stains.

March 1940

LE REVENANT AGAIN

I could spend all my evenings walking with you
Along those woodland roads, our eager talk
Ranging from Trotsky to the old Greek gods,
While spring's young vigour thrilled us heavenwards.

And those my new-found friends, so hale and simple,
Who smile and patronise, do they understand,
When they laugh at my memory vague, my hair a-yangle,
 – Could they ever understand? – how I despise
The limited virtues which they've always trusted,
And only long to be with you a while,
The warm the wild the towsled and the twisted?

New Herrlingen School, 25th March 1940

NIKOLAI GOGOL

On whose tomb are the words "I shall laugh my bitter laugh."
    Yes, I shall laugh my bitter madman's laugh
And wander dismally from town to town
While in the market by the golden calf
The petty-hearted squabble cheat and clown,
Drowned in their shallow mire of lusts and fears.
    Yes, I shall laugh my bitter laugh
And raise a grin from every fool that hears.
Yea laughable the twisted misery,
The dirt, the drunken blurred paralysis,
And the sad sight of man's nobility
Crossing its sword with fate's injustices,
Doomed to disaster through the changeless years.
    Yea I shall laugh my bitter laugh
And draw a veil of smiles to hide my tears.
And you whom most I hate, the placid bores
Who sit at home and sip your sweetened tea
And drawl that this is no affair of yours,
    – Think you to vegetate eternally
Untroubled by the malice of my jeers?
    Nay. I shall laugh my bitter laugh
Until its frenzied echo haunts your ears!
March 1940

NEKYIA

Now is the barque of Charon filled to creaking;
Full-crowded too the Stygian banks forlorn.
Only a helpless fluttering and squeaking
Recalls to us the men of yestermorn.
Demos and Oligarch, – whoever rule
These cities and heap the searing fires,
Is not a man a thing more beautiful
Than all the tarnished gold of our desires?
10 April 1940

*(Note: On this day came the news of the loss of two
British warships, and the troopship Bremen with 1300 men on board.)*

AGUIST APOLLON EMOS

*Written after a lorry had grazed the back-plate of my
motor-bike, both of us travelling at 30 miles an hour.*

Shooting out of the sun
    Through a chilling wind of death,
I woke too late to act
    – Just gripped and held my breath.

One second and it passed.
    I shuddered and rode on.
Too long a time to face
    My keen apollyon.

God of the ways my destroyer,
    I'm sorry you were baulked.
The gun was sighted truly.
    The game was fairly stalked.

Sunlight to sunlight cheating
    The swift black death that swerved,
Whom do I thank for life
    Unhoped for, underserved?
                17th April 1940

WINTER SUNLIGHT

This is the tense time: steelbright, cheerless
The sun looks on: like leafless trees
The nerves stand bare: tiresome the words drip
Wearing a crease down limbs: restless the wind.
The fat man plays the fool and enjoys it hugely.
The brainless woman chatters expecting praise.

For me two things are true.
    – Hatred, vivid as the bracken,
Crackling and sere: the other, a thundercloud,
Sultry and black with no clear focus,
Sulking in every vein, my sick desire.
                1940

LEISURE-LOVE

Because I was cool when the angry dogstar struck us,
You threaten to leave for more responsive fires.
Well? I have seen too much of blackthorn by moonlight
To be so wholly the fool of my desires.

Because I stalled. At that high engine-speed
My driving wheels seized up and would not move.
I have walked too long through water-meadows in summer
To be so serious about love.

I'm still uncertain about the truth of living.
From so many answers I must yet find one
That slots in easily and needs no oiling.
And even then my search will not be done.

But one thing's clear. Your formula will not suit me.
This heat's destruction was not for you and me.
There is still the challenge of cowslips under hedges.
There is still the critical murmur of the sea.

                                        22nd April 1940

TO IRUSHKA

When I can find the time between sleep and working,
Between hard earth and the cold morning air,
Or a longer rest in the sunlight basking,
I like to remember the gentle things that were.

The tireless novelty of age-grey cities,
The tabby cat asleep with folded paws,
Cornfields too conscious of their beauties
 — All these bring sense and freshness to my cause.

But one thing taunts me out of all this kindness;
 — With the peaceful eyes and soothing hair,
Stand to the barricades beside us!
Then I would die today and hardly care.

                                        5th July 1940

MISSUNS (*AENEID* VI)

Flotsam you found me where the gulls were wheeling,
Brackish with brine – your friend, whose laughter
Soared up and circled high above despair,
Kept your hearts ticking over through disaster,
But would not stay to triumph – and you said sadly
"This man whom all the Danaans could not cow,
Has fallen now to his own wildness,
Calling the waves to contest madly."

Was it so wild? You know I never longed
To conquer right or wrong. I could not learn
To strut uneasy through unfriendly cities.
How would I fit? In this new venture
Of listless men whose demon will not rest
O offer one thing concrete – me
Flaunting my crimson robes defiant,
Clenching my sword and trumpet, tamed by the sea.

3rd August 1940

ICH HATT' EINEN KAMARADEN [6]

We were together when we marked our goal,
Shooting beyond the mountains of desire,
Then sadly shook our heads – "They sped
Too wild and high. They will be hard to trace."
And then we laughed. – Together we shall find
Fixed gleaming in the meadowland behind
Our arrows marking out for us a place.

Together we watched hope come winging inland
Craning her neck with gay barbaric cries,
Then sadly shook our heads – "She fled
Too far and fast. She cannot be pursued."
And then we laughed. – Together we shall break
Through to the unfathomable lake
Where now she rides at anchor with her brood.

17th August 1940

ALLOTRIAS DIAI GUNAIKOS (*AGAMEMNON* 437-451)[7]

Between the dartboard and the empty fireplace
They are talking now of the boys the village has lost;
Tom, our best bowler all last season,
Died clean and swift as he lived, when his plane went reeling;
Bill, who drank beer and laughed, is now asleep
Behind Dunkerque, helped others to escape;
And Dave went down on that aircraft carrier,
Dave, whom nobody minded,
But who played the flute rather well, I remember.

    "Those boys died bravely. We'll always be proud of them.
    They've given old Adolf something to set him thinking."
    That was the loudest, the driving wave of opinion.
    But in the corner hear the eddies singing –
    "Allotrias diai gunaikos." [8]

"Helen the Fair went over the water
With Paris your friend, one of your own gang,
Whom we never trusted, but you feasted,
For years with fawning, let your lands go hang.
We warned you. You could have stopped it.
But now we have sent our sons from the cornfields.
War, like a grocer, weights and sends us back
Ashes for men and all our year goes black."

    "Yes. They died well, but not to suit your purpose;
    Not so that you could go hunting with two horses,
    While their sons touched their caps, opening the gates for
    pennies.
    Perhaps we shall take a hand, write our own ending."
    Tade siga tis bauzei.[9]

                        August 1940

24

LONELINESS

Quickly exchanging glances with their eyes
That flashed as we marched forward, you believed
That comradeship was all? At halting-time,
Joking and singing, knocking the tankards down,
You called it perfect union, - looked to live
Warmed by their sympathy and hoped your mind
When ill would just relax
Smooth-cushioned on the folds of his or hers
Until the fever left? Was that your dream?

They who had nerves to fight, humor to laugh,
And blood to feel, – how could they waste an hour
On your neurotic grief? Let them go on!
Drag yourself like a leopard to the hills
And lick your sores in peace. Learn like the cat,
The stately cat, soft-prowling through the grass,
Silent and proud, to stalk and think alone.

                              18th November 1940

III TWO TRANSLATIONS FROM THE RUSSIAN

DO NOT SAY "HE DIED"

Translated from the Russian of S.Y. Nadson[10]

Nay. Do not say "he died". He is alive.
Quench ye the altar-fire? – It flames again.
Pluck ye the rose? – Again its flowers thrive.
Shattered the lyre? – The sobbing chords remain.

12th April 1940

YA VAS LYUBIL

(from Pushkin)

I loved you once. Who knows but even now
Love in my soul may not be wholly dead?
But never let it trouble you. I vow
I would not hurt you by a thing I did.

I loved you once in silent desperation.
Shyness and envy wrecked me numb with pain.
I loved you once. God grant such adoration
So true, so gentle, comes your way again!

IV POEMS 1941–1943

A POEM ON THE COMING SPRING

This is the time of ice-floe-cracking,
Freedom to fjord and harbour. Now the bear
Stumps from his mountain-lair above the Vardar
Nosing the growth-smell. Crocuses break snow
In all the Alps, and Greece is flower-starr'd.
Here in England the change comes milder
And frost unclenches slowly: flaunting his yellow
Head on the hill the hazel looks a leader
To straggling junipers: softly the willow
Slips on her sealskin mittens: everywhere
Nature is glad of the creative season,
But man, Wise Man, waits helpless with despair.

Spring frees the harbours for destruction,
Spring looses tanks across the plain,
Spring, after winter's interruption,
Kindles the Holokaust again.
Spring the city-flattener,
Spring the man's blood battener,
Spring of the million graves,
Spring of the wreck-strewn waves,
Gas-spring, bomber-spring,
Spring that is no spring,
Only a rotten thing
Pregnant with richer slaughter than last year.

                              25th February 1941.

"BROTHER"

Naked, naked the larches
Marching with vacant slowness on the down
Frown without friends, nor know for all their closeness
Love's unity, the warm collaboration
Of oak and hazel. Only in themselves
They find their strength and their frustration.

They keep aloof, my comrade, my brother from you
And others, not of our blood, but brothers too
With whom our roots are locked. Why is the hill
Larch-lonely, split with hostile coppices?
Why is there limit set on our good will?
Make this our task — out of a time-stained word
Often invoked but rarely true, to weld
A slogan that will galvanise the world.

                                        8th March 1941

MARATHANOMAKH

To Nikoteles the Sophist, now the sun
Is cropping clover on Hymettus, I send
These words by the friend who will soon pull down my eyelids,
The last words I shall speak in Attika.

I call to mind, Nikoteles, our walks
In the olive-yards, the many things we discussed
And the clever remarks we made — in particular
About Life, which seemed a strange puzzle
Whose point we could not find, — and our similes
Of the fat sailor spitting in the fish-market,
Farouche but full of interest, December rain
Soaking the finger bones or the lute-player
Who was drunk and only rarely played good music.
Often we branded it mellow but quite empty
Like a lovely flower that has no pollen.
You were fond of saying that only a dying man
Could give a balanced judgement: for that reason
I hope to amuse you with these observations.

You will get, I'm afraid, no witty sophist answer,
Sharp and one-sided — "Life is a comic play
Which those in the pit enjoy" — "a tragedy
Too sordid to be fine" — "a school" — "a struggle".
Nor can you graft on nature a suspicion
Of point or purpose: that is a human twist
Foreign to life: on this green fennel-field

As the numbness spreads from my feet upwards,
I see it clearly – Life is movement and growth,
All that is real – Death is not what we hoped,
Not restful, but obscurantist, a foul smoke
That blinds and chokes - growth is supremely good
And in itself an end. Of all my years
I only regret the hours spent dozing in porches
After drinking too much wine, the argument
Shirked out of laziness, the stifled question.

You, Nikoteles, if the gods are kind,
Will spend many years in that strange city of Athens,
Which none of us understand, you will watch the folk
Taking their evening airing on the Pnyx
Or greeting the asphodels on Lykabettos.
You will see, no doubt, a great deal more of destruction
And as much as you can of spring. If you have time
You will probably stop to pose our favourite problem,
"Why?" – but remember "Why?" is academic,
Irrelevant to life. Do you think the olive
Asks "Why?" before budding out? Does the fennel ask it?
When you stretch yourself on the dry-scented hillside
And stare at Salamis, – leave off asking "Why?"
Remember what I, your friend, on my deathbed saw –
When I died at Marathon, I saw this only:
By my head the fennel was growing, slowly.
                                13th March 1941

   REX

A word from England brought you back to mind,
Oldest of friends, and how we walked together
From Foxcombe round by Cumnor in the kind
Celandine season or, in harebell weather
When haws glow crisp from hedges – dogs that were lost
In long grass hunting rabbits, solemn talk
Of school and coming college, till the last
Visit to Sunningwell, when we tarried,
Liking the churchyard and its yew-dark grass,
Where, if they tell the truth, you now lie buried.
                                June 1941

SOLILOQUY IN A GREEK CLOISTER

Lover of cypresses, a friend of death,
With fierce black beard, weak mouth, a drunkard's eyes,
Nikephoros, a priest of the Greek faith,
I watch the melons grow and water them:
Then the hills lengthen and the crickets wake.

Tomorrow, as the melons are in order,
The quinces not yet ripe, apricots over,
I'll climb the Holy Peak, making excuse
Our need for hyssop. Shaded near the top
I'll sit the day and watch the hot red hills
Struggle and seethe and toss, the camel tracks
Thread their thin way between, the vultures wheel
Intransigent above. I'll dream, perhaps,
Much of the future, something of the past.

Here it is pleasant, a regret comes rarely –
– Only when pilgrims call. – Once in five years
One scans my face and stops – "Wait. I remember,
"In the City some years back – Was it at Court?
And a party on the Bosphoros by moonlight?
Or riding up in Thrace. What is your name?
"What is your story, brother?" I reply.
"I know too well the great Romaic city.
I too am Greek and proud. Now I live here,
Nikephoros, am orthodox in faith,
With fierce black beard, weak mouth, a drunkard's eyes,
Lover of cypresses, a friend of Death."

                                    5th August 1941

ISKANDAR BIL KARNEIN*

Iskandar, a hard-drinking, dominant man,
A beautiful master of horses, tamed the world,
Conquered a bride, grew ram's horns like Great Zeus,
Founded a queenly city and then died.

Strike for the sea-road; take the coolest street
Down to the white-washed mosque by Spiro's shop:
Ask for Iskandar: tell them, "He is here
Deep in some vault recumbent, roaring still
In Macedonian orgy, hurling down
His empty tankards like a god in pain."
Shrugly they'll answer, "Iskandar is not here.
Where he is gone one only understands.
Seek him at sunset in his vague domain –
The cynic daimon of the Libyan sands."

11th August 1941

*Alexander of the Double Horns.

DE AMICITIA [11]

Odysseus, at the end of life, in your orchards,
Stroking the olive-flowers and the young corn
With thin dry fingers – only in your eyes
The fire that once was the whole man – Odysseus,
Tell me, from all your travels
What do you most remember?

"Not Troy, not any thought of Troy.
Not Polypheme. Not Kalypso. Nor does the sea
Feature except as a well-honoured friend
Smiling a greeting but no invitation.

"More than all else I think of the Phaeacians,
Leisure and music in their halls,
The laughter of Alkinous and his tales,
The freedom and the peace of an old friendship,

And Nausikaa,
    gay as hibiscus-bloom,
Fresher than dawn, shining unconscious foil
To my other world, to all the dross of manhood."

24th April 1942

AUBADE [12]

...

Hullo, Brian! Writing to you from Persia,
Here is a picture that you would have liked.

Morning. North, on the snow mountains,
Black thunder-clouds. Shifting across the slopes,
Shadow and sunlight ring their changes;
Subtle and swift; unsure; illusory.
But look below! The poplars of the plain
Gay and erect like tall Udarniks stride,
Bronzed by the autumn, lissom, challenging,
And do not know defeat. Over their heads
White pigeons wheel, gracefully, thoughtfully,
Rise and descend, etched clear against the clouds.
Catch and fling back the sunlight from their wings.

This is your landscape, Brian. This was your life.
Thunder and cloudburst only brought you strength,
Steeled your fine spirit. Brave were all your ways,
Straighter than poplars, and your airborne thoughts
Wheeled high above, defying the dark clouds
And, from their wings, reflecting
Glory, that we, who cannot make such flights,
Are not forgetting.

November 1942

POLLICITI MELIORA [13]
(Epitaph for my friends.)

As one who, gazing at a vista
    Of beauty, sees the clouds close in,
And turns his back in sorrow, hearing
    The thunderclouds begin,

So we, whose life was all before us,
    Our hearts with sunlight filled,
Left in the hills our books and flowers,
    Descended and were killed.

Write on the stones no words of sadness —
    Only the gladness due,
That we, who asked the most of living,
    Knew how to give it, too.

                    1942?

REQUIESCAT IN PACE [14]

Silenced by well-hid sniper
he spreadeagled the slit-trench bottom.

Shed no tears for him, for
he has a resting-place of panoramic view
carefully sited
tactically sound
with excellent field of fire.

For him
no quick-tossed clods of earth
to press him into nothingness.

He shall be exposed
to all the changing seasons
and the gentle soothing rain
and he shall lie at peace — forever.

Or at least, until
the War Graves people
bag him up
move him on.

                    1942/43 ?

TENT-PITCHERS[15]

This is the third day of the khamsin,
The fierce, monotonous insistence
Of hot dry blast, silting up eyes and hair,
Taut-straining the frayed guy-ropes of resistance.
Heat thick enough to cut. Wind but no air.

Two swaddies pitching tent in the full sun,
Tugging the bellying canvas down,
Stripped to the waist, hair matted, eyes, back, chest
Caked in a sweaty plaster, shake their heads.
"Well, Bill? Yer glad yer came out East?"
"Ho yuss! I wouldn't have missed this for quids!"

O England! Oh my lovely casual country!
These are your lads, English as blackthorn flower,
Bearing your freshness with them, facing each hour,
Desert or death, with the same free unstudied
Serenity of meadowland in April –
Carelessly littered with fritillaries,
Ladysmock, kingcups, cowslips, and wild apple!
                    June 1943

38

SONNET

Luke 9/24

I have always loved men who were spendthrifts,
Whose ways were prodigal as the sea-waves
Crashing it out in the roar and spindrift,
A million ecstasies, a million graves;

Or whose hearts were wide as the desert,
As quiet under the stars, as clear and strong;
Though convoys pass without purpose, dazzled,
Winds wailing scatter the traces when they're gone.

For these there is no frustration,
Asphyxiation of aspidistra rooms,
The merciless, the mad boredom of possession,
The cupboards crammed with junk, cluttered with crumbs.

Our new Franciscan oath, clerk's vow or king's –
Let us be free from the tyranny of things!

1943?

V AN ECLOGUE OF NEMESIS

AN ECLOGUE OF NEMESIS

Ubique

Corydon.

A stranger.

"It seems so strange. I had toyed with the thought of dying
Often, with morbid pleasure, but never like this.
Not here! Not now, like a beetle crushed by a cartwheel!
My death should have been a gesture of lordliness.

With friends by my side, I'd have carolled a last dirge,
Searching and tender; dedicated my flute
In the old traditional style to Pan or Lykaion;
Then passed in splendour to silence absolute.

Then would the country have darkened at my going.
Then men would have said "Shall we hear such songs again
As Corydon sang in the evening among the foxgloves."
My name would have lasted, – a sweetness flecked with pain.

Death chose his own way. Shrunk and black with plague,
I face him now; and not a friend will dare
Stand by to close my eyelids. My hands have lost
The strength to lift the pipes for one last air.

Not here! Not now! In another year or two
I should be famous for the songs I sing.
Now no one knows my name except my village,
And they'll forget me with the coming spring.

Galatea, perhaps, will mourn me till the summer;
But young Alexis waits. Before June's ended
She'll lie by his side. June's far too hot a time
To rest a widow. How long will my grave be tended?

But they will remember always, the furry people
That rustle and bob on hill and brackened glen.
And the trees and the bracken itself and the honeysuckle?
Surely these keep a stronger faith than men.

Surely they'll think of me, when the dogstar's fiercest,
– Of times I would lie, on the bank with my drowsy sheep
And pipe them my songs, not polished, but sweet and soothing,
Till every leaf and insect sank asleep.

And then, when the moon laughs down and the woods grow
        lively,
And the rabbits dance by the path where the beech-trees end,
They'll think of the time I stood quietly by and watched them.
They'll see my place empty, and know they have lost a friend.

Sure they'll remember. – What is that to me,
When the grass and the nettles are dancing above my head?
I shall be dead. There's no philosophy
Will comfort a young man dying. I'll be dead."

"– No. There's no comfort, shepherd. I'll not cheat you.
I'll tread your hopes to matchwood, roughly shod.
Soon you will be a smudge upon death's blackboard.
Alive, you had the chance to be a god."

"Alive, I was a god. But who are you?
I've seen you before, I think, these last grim days,
Gloating above my bed, your dark blue cloak
Shrouding your shoulders, malignant eyes ablaze.

Now's the first time you've spoken, and harsh words, too,
Echoing only the dregs of my despair.
Are you a demon from Tartarus to taunt me
Or only fever's phantasy? Speak! Don't stare!"

"No demon, shepherd. No fevered apparition.
You have read your poets, shepherd, and know them well?"
"I've read their stories closely, and I found
No tragedy like mine in what they tell."

"Have you heard them tell of Nemesis, the Avenger,
Who snatches her victims suddenly, ruthlessly?"

42

"I've often heard of her, but never feared her.
I never incurred her anger."
                              "I am she."

"I begin to understand
 Things I had not believed,
 Refused to believe, because of my buoyant strength,
 My faith in all I loved.
 The old historian from Halikarnassos
 Had grasped the truth in its simplicity,
 'Divinity is jealous', and I
 Was too alive to see.

 Too late I know the truth
 At which my body rebelled.
 The grand poetic lies are torn and scattered,
 Their foolishness revealed.
 They were all false, then, those genealogies
 Of Koros, Hybris, Ate and the rest,
 And Nemesis is envy simply
 Against earth's happiest.

 Guilty for daring to live
 In a land where Death was lord,
 To be gay among men whose hearts were clogged with dullness,
 I pay the price incurred.
 Because I let life's sordidness flow by me
 And played one clear unwavering song,
 And set my heart on beauty only,
 My way of life was wrong.

 Doomed to eternal surfeit,
 How could the jaded gods
 Stand by and watch me radiant in my youth,
 Indiff'rent to their goads?
 And I lived on in rustic calm, not fearing
 The swift reactions of their angry hate,
 Until their thunder struck, and left me
 In ashes desolate.

"A smudge on death's cold blackboard
Soon wiped to nothingness.
Seaweed floating by the shore of Lethe
Soon dragged to the abyss.
I who was once called Corydon the Cheerful,
Who claimed to have found a peace denied to most,
Am brought to this by heaven's envy
Made livid at my boast."

"You're young. You're a fool, shepherd,
To think you count so high.
You're young, to groan so loud for personal justice
In the world's misery.
Were there in heaven such discrimination,
Your self-importance still would claim its own.
You would deserve to perish almost
For this conceit alone.

No, not the observations
Of neatly posted gods,
No careful calculations ever furnish
Fate's batteries with guides.
Impersonal, with general application
Of nature's laws, their barrage sweeps the ground.
No peace, nor any safety, shepherd,
Within their range is found.

In a land where Death was master,
You lived and did not care.
Though you walked among men whose hearts were cold with
sickness,
You tried to find no cure.
And yet you moan and whine, when you fall victim,
Calling the envy of the gods to blame.
Yet Nemesis seems only justice
Called by a grimmer name."

"Yes. There is fairness here. I was hypnotised
Too wholly by the light of my own vision.
And yet it still seems harsh. I was a poet.

How could I have the power to turn physician?
Could I not heal in my own way with music,
Flinging the notes abroad for all to hear?
Or was not that a worthy contribution
– To keep my song harmonious and clear?"

"Yours was a rootless travesty of clearness,
When all around was discord and distress.
You should have sung for others. You should have felt
More than the whims of your own shallowness.

You were a moth, shepherd, in a room at night-time,
Dazed by your won bright-flamed nobility.
You never glanced at the shadows in the corners
Or even questioned far their entity.

You were a swallow by a lake in summer,
Brushing the water with a careless wing.
How should you know what lurked beneath the ripples?
Air was the element where you were king.

You should have felt, good shepherd, you should have questioned.
No more was asked. But you could only dote
On your own beauty. Had you known more feeling,
Your music would have found a truer note."

"And so it seems my way of life was wasted.
Even this comfort leaves me at last.
And I must sink to earth a man rejected,
Whom even his own fields and hills outcast.

When the rooks gather in the elms at sunset,
They'll caw and laugh at Corydon the vain,
And Corydon will rouse the jay's mad chatter,
Till all the woods re-echo with my pain.

"No! I rebel! Not wasted! There were moments
That had a beauty timeless and serene,
Were in themselves an end; and others shared them.
These are the things that flourish evergreen.

Men will remember Corydon the dreamer
And say "He gave us brittle songs but good."
They will be thankful then for what I taught them,
— Some joy expressed, some beauty understood."

"Take, if you like, that solace on your journey.
But you, and nobler men than you, are dead.
In your hands was the power to save disaster.
Your death and theirs lie heavy on your head.

These laws were made of old, enduring, changeless,
And must pursue their course relentlessly.
I, even I, can only stand and watch
Their havoc through the ages helplessly."

The footnotes which accompany the poems are the author's.
We have not attempted to explain the classical references which are
present in most of the poems.

1. The title is a line from the poem "Heidenröslein" by Goethe. The
   concept of untouched beauty in Goethe's "Morgenschön" is
   difficult to translate into English.
2. Title translation: 'Why do you ask me to sing?'
3. Irushka was Iris Murdoch
4. *Le Revenant* is usually translated into English as 'ghost'. Here it
   rather carries the sense of a spirit returning to its past life. There
   is no word in modern English for this exact meaning, although
   the word 'revenant' was sometimes used in the past.
5. This poem was published in Victor Selwyn (ed.), *The Voice of
   War: Poems of the Second World War*, Penguin Press 1996.
6. The title – 'I had a Comrade' – is that of a German folksong and
   marching song which tells the story of a soldier whose comrade
   in arms is killed fighting at his side.
7. Title translation: 'They died in a war of others' making'. This was
   published in *For your tomorrow: an anthology of poetry by young men
   from English public schools who fell in the World War 1939 – 1945*,
   Oxford University Press 1950.
8. Translation: 'They died in a war of others' making'.
9. Translation: 'Soft but the Titan heard it singing'.
10. S.Y. Nadson (1862-1887), popular 'civic' poet, admirer of
    Neerasov, wrote of the evils of despotism and social injustice.
    Died very young of consumption.
11. 'Friendship'. First published in *For your tomorrow*.
12. A song for the morning – written in memory of Brian Carritt,
    who had recently died.
13. The title means literally 'Having promised better things'. The
    poem was published in both *For your tomorrow* and *The Voice
    of War,* and was read at the ceremonies to commemorate V-E
    day and V-Day in 1995.
14. Title translation: 'May he rest in Peace'. Published in *The Voice
    of War.*
15. Published in *For your tomorrow.*